living room
essentials

JUDITH WILSON

living room
essentials

RYLAND
PETERS
& SMALL
LONDON NEW YORK

Designer Emilie Ekström
Editors Clare Double and Sophie Bevan
Picture research Claire Hector and Emily Westlake
Production Louise Bartrum
Art Director Gabriella Le Grazie
Publishing Director Alison Starling

ISBN 1-84172-479-3

10 9 8 7 6 5 4 3 2 1

First published in the United Kingdom
in 2003 by Ryland Peters & Small
Kirkman House
12–14 Whitfield Street
London W1T 2RP
www.rylandpeters.com

Text copyright © Judith Wilson and
Ryland Peters & Small 2003
Design and photographs copyright
© Ryland Peters & Small 2003

A CIP record for this book is available from the British Library.

Printed and bound in China

contents

getting the

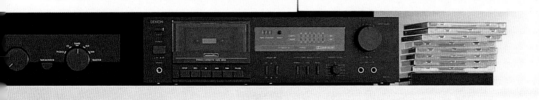

elements right

planning the space

For the lucky few, the living room is a tranquil space for winding down and a cool style statement in terms of objects and furniture. But for the majority it is the nerve centre of the home, where family life, TV-watching and socializing coexist, day in, day out. The living room is a harder-working room than most of us realize, so begin by asking yourself some salient questions. How much time will be spent there, and what activities will go on there? What favourite possessions do you want to show off? What needs to be stored? Can the room be rearranged for entertaining?

Far left Even a subtle shift in furniture style or colour – plastics versus leather, primaries contrasted with neutrals – can separate areas without compromising the spirit of an open-plan living space.

Left In a narrow living room, several upholstered dining chairs, rather than bulky armchairs, provide ad hoc seating without cluttering the space.

Above and below Add essential intimacy to a large living area by clustering chairs and sofas into sociable groups.

• this is probably the hardest-working room in your home, so **make a list** of all the functions you require of it

• for **careful space management**, draw up a plan of your room and cut out scale shapes to represent your furnishings

• a real or real-effect fire creates a **natural focal point** and is always worth the investment

• **plan where the technology will go** at the outset to ensure the TV, stereo, etc can be housed both practically and tidily

Left and far left Dual-purpose furnishings – a coffee table with drawers, cupboards which offer display and storage – help a room design to work harder. Right If dimensions are tight, create an optical illusion with slim, 'barely there' furniture. Below right In an open-plan space, a table behind the sofa provides a visual and practical division of zones.

Correct furniture arrangement is paramount. Good planning means you can watch TV in comfort, chat easily with friends, and may even squeeze in enough room for a separate seating area for quiet reading or card games. If there is a natural focal point in the room, be it a fireplace or a great view, it can be a useful decorative starting point. It sounds a cliché, but drawing a scale plan of the room and cutting out to-scale shapes of existing furniture really will help. In terms of human traffic flow, remember that space between furniture always seems less once translated into three dimensions, so err on the generous side.

Good lighting can make or break a living room. If possible, replace central pendant lighting, as it casts ugly shadows. But don't do away with overhead lighting altogether – every living room needs the option of bright light sometimes, and don't forget task lights for reading. Plan for plenty of side lights, too, and put all lights on a dimmer switch.

Controlling natural light is equally important. If sunlight is too dazzling, consider screening it with blinds or ' shutters. If the room is naturally shady, place at least one chair and table next to a window to capitalize on daylight.

colour schemes

When choosing the colours of your living room, go classic. A neutral colour scheme provides the best backdrop for pretty possessions, furnishings and artworks, and is easily updated with fresh splashes of colour. In addition, it actively detracts from an obvious trend or date of furniture. A wing chair, in dark paisley, is 'period', whereas the same chair upholstered in white cotton is simply a pretty shape that blends easily with other styles in the room.

Left Inexpensive, ready-made curtains are a wonderful way to ring the changes with new colour. If choosing sheers, remember that even the brightest of shades will be diluted by strong sunlight.

Above The most utilitarian of storage pieces, from a simple cabinet to built-in units, can be a colour statement. Spray-painted doors create a sleek, professional finish.

Far left and right Focus attention on a bright artwork by keeping the rest of the room quietly neutral. Even a plain painted artist's canvas can be used to 'lift' a tired scheme, adding fresh colours each season.

Choose upholstery in cool tones, from white to deep graphite, and furniture in wood, metal or rattan. Then apply this palette to smaller items, from ceramic lamp bases to stone platters, glass vases and oak photo frames. If there are wooden floorboards, consider sisal, jute or neutral-coloured wool rugs.

Now you are ready to bring colour and pattern into play. Whether it's a single large piece, like an armchair upholstered in tangerine denim, or several smaller items, such as shell-pink side tables, the point to remember is that the colours should be easy and inexpensive to change. Look out for sale-bargain fabrics or furniture that can be repainted. If a patterned or coloured piece is to last, make sure you love it in its own right as opposed to tying it into a complete coordinated scheme. One armchair upholstered in green chintz will look good with a white sofa, or – five years on – with a grey one; it is only when the chintz has been matched to other elements, such as chairs and curtains, that problems arise.

Of course, we don't all want to live in a neutral space, so if you love colour then put it on the walls. Remember that your chosen shades will deeply affect the room's ambience: off-pastels are soothing; bright blocks stimulating; and deep, sombre tones sophisticated yet warm. As your sitting room is

Top Lift plain upholstery with detailing such as buttoning or a contrast piping.
Above A bright, generous throw is a useful trick for adding instant colour to a tired sofa, though its informality works best in a more traditional setting.
Right Choosing to upholster a single piece in a bright shade may seem self-indulgent, but it adds a novel twist to an otherwise classic scheme.
Far right Plan coloured upholstery with imagination. A piece needn't always be all one colour. Find a creative upholsterer and ask for mix-and-match two-tone plains for a truly individual look.

Above left Dark wood panelling creates a particularly sophisticated background for bright flashes of upholstery.
Above right A multicoloured rug allows you to pick out key tones in upholstery or accessories.
Far left Leather comes in a surprisingly varied choice of colours, from pastels to brights.
Left Amass a 'wardrobe' of cushions with which to change a neutral scheme each season.

- wall **texture radically affects colour** – matt paint or wool felt walling will deepen a shade, whereas eggshell or sparkly papers will lighten it

- **create a colour board** – complete with fabric, paint and flooring samples – and examine it in different lights

- colours needn't match exactly; it is more crucial to **get the tonal balance right**

- **think big** – paint huge boards or borrow large fabric samples to get the full effect of a colour, rather than rely on tiny chips and swatches

the chief entertaining space – and a design statement for visitors – be a little more daring. If it's a room primarily used by night, choose dramatic colours that look good in artificial light. Picking elegant pastels, by contrast, will deliberately set apart a more formal living room from a family den.

Even braver is to put blocks of colour onto the floor or as window treatments. It gives a chic, pulled-together look, though the disadvantage is that if you tire of the colour it's an expensive mistake to rectify. So be realistic. Pale light-reflecting floor shades are tempting, but will require constant cleaning, whereas a vivid colour may 'fight' with other possessions, causing you to heavily edit favourite things. Many interior designers stick to the golden rule of choosing only earth colours for the floor, from green to ochre, never an unnatural sky blue. Remember, too, that strong-coloured curtains will create a disruptive contrasting block against the walls. Choosing both in the same shade is more soothing.

Opposite A splash of colour, in the form of a painting or fabric pattern, in an all-white interior looks striking. Here, the harsh contrast is softened by choosing curvy, rather than straight, outlines for the furniture.

Above left Wall colour needn't be uniform. If painting surfaces yourself, bands of graded colour, passing from dark to light, create a particularly dramatic effect.

Left In a naturally dark room or a space mostly used at night, pick stronger, muted colours that look good in dim light. Plums, graphite and moss green are good choices.

Above Look for finishes that improve with age – leather, plaster moulding, gilding, foxed mirrors and antique wood are all good choices.

Left Often the most interesting living rooms result from a mix of styles and materials. Yet, if you're nervous of combining the unexpected, try to pick a theme. Choosing lots of furniture with skinny legs, for example, looks funky and fun. Alternatively, try all curved pieces together or a preponderance of boxy silhouettes.

furniture &
soft furnishings

Choosing a style for the furnishing of your living room is the exciting part, but give great thought to your budget. A living room demands investment pieces, from sofas to bookshelves, not to mention metres of fabric and the almost ruinous cost of making up soft furnishings. It can be an expensive business, so try to compose a classic scheme which will endure and can be updated with trendier accessories.

This page Newly fashionable, the modular sofa has particular benefits. If your budget is tight, investing in a combination of stool, daybed and corner pieces could be more cost-effective than buying the conventional sofa plus two armchairs. Great for small spaces, because of its streamlined outline, it's also one of the most relaxed seating options you can pick, perfect both for socializing and sprawling.

Left When choosing furniture styles, think carefully about how you use the living room. Do you prefer to sit up and chat, or chill out horizontally? If the latter, a daybed or long, lean sofa is a crucial choice, as are armchairs with angled backs. Never be afraid to try out furniture in the shop, as it's the only way to pick for comfort. **Below** If you prefer over-stuffed upholstery and plump cushions, pick a sofa with a sufficiently deep seat, so there's room for you and the cushions.

The first step in selecting your furnishings is to look at what you have. A sofa may be reupholstered in a new fabric, or a battered side table given a new, distressed paint finish. Ask yourself pertinent questions in order to refine your needs. If you entertain frequently, would two small sofas be better than one large model? Might a daybed suit the room more than an armchair? And a coffee table isn't a necessity if four small side tables will do the job just as well. Think, too, about the practicality and quality of each piece you choose. Although the living room may be used only during evenings or at weekends, its major components need to last at least a decade. So buy the best you can afford, and put your money into the most heavily used pieces. The main sofa should have coil-sprung

Above left It's easy to focus on major furniture choices, but pay due attention to the smaller items, from side tables to lamps. Ensure they perform well on a practical level, as well as look good.
Above, centre and right However plain the chosen look, it's fun to add zest with unusually styled upholstery or soft furnishings. Good options are contrast stitching or simple borders on cushions, and lacing, studding or buttoning on upholstered items.
Below For a streamlined look, remember to choose pieces that are on a similar level: low-slung sofas demand equally low storage cabinets.

seats and duck-feather-filled cushions, but you could go for foam upholstery on an occasional armchair. There's nothing wrong with veneered wood furniture, but check the quality, as some cheap veneers are very fragile. If possible, choose solid wood for a table that will see lots of use. Opt for real metals instead of a metal-effect finish, which may chip.

The key to choosing successful furnishings is versatility. Any of the major pieces will involve a substantial outlay, even a high-street sofa, so you need to know that when, in five years' time, the walls are repainted another colour, the furniture will still be going strong, even though small details may need tweaking. It's therefore important to pick designs that can reflect fresh looks. Pick sofas with pretty legs and

an elegant silhouette, giving you the option of choosing plump upholstery or loose covers. Simple, inexpensive MDF or wood pieces can be repainted in different colours. And think of smaller items – console tables or a side chair – as the equivalents of those skirts and trousers that mix and match with the key suit jacket. If attractive in their own right, they can also be moved around the house for visual variety.

In terms of design, there are certain failsafe styles for the sitting room. For upholstery, many classics are still the best. You can't go far wrong with the wing chair or, for a more modern look, a boxy sofa, both of which not only boast a great outline but also look good with antique or contemporary pieces. Ignore clumsy or overly fussy designs with puffy cushions. When choosing tables or cabinets, stick to simple styling in quality materials, and mix curvy and rectangular shapes together. However, don't get hung up on classics at the expense of indulging your personal style. Let that shine through in one or two unusual pieces.

- a living room demands **investment pieces**, so go for a classic scheme that will last – thus spreading the cost

- **dual-purpose furniture**, such as a coffee table with drawers or a dining-cum-work table, helps a living room work harder

- **luxurious upholstery** that also wears well includes wool mixes, linen or chenille. Save silk, satin or suede for occasional chairs

- **cover cushions or a small chair** in a fabric you adore – it will look almost as good as an entire sofa upholstered in the fabric, but is much less expensive

Opposite Don't fall into the trap of buying 'classic' furniture, only to end up with a room that looks like your parents'. Stay true to your style, but add a sophisticated spin for the living room. So, if you like beanbags, pick them in vinyl or leather. Shabby-chic fans can go for a distressed antique mirror in place of a newly gilded one. And, whatever your style, ensure you have the cushions you love.
This page Fresh upholstery can transform a second-hand sofa or armchair. Pick neutrals to give you free rein for pretty cushions, or a patterned fabric to turn a chair into a strong focal point.

This page Choose translucent blinds in a sunny room to encourage dramatic light-play, as well as to screen rays. Plain blinds, pierced with holes, create particularly pretty effects.
Opposite left A Roman blind, with its flat panel, is one of the best ways to show off patterned fabric at windows. Always line blinds, as they hang better and it prevents show-through from fittings on the back.
Opposite right A fitted sheer panel conceals an ugly view more decoratively than net curtains.

window treatments

The perfect window treatment needs to be functional as well as look stylish. A good curtain or blind will filter strong sunlight, provide privacy, even protect against chills, not to mention screening a less than enviable urban view. At the same time, window treatments offer myriad decorative opportunities. They can become a focal point in the absence of an architecturally interesting window frame, they can highlight a great view or can show off a beautiful fabric.

When deciding on window treatments, give due attention to the shape and size of the windows, the light flow and the view. Consider, too, whether to choose blinds or curtains. On the whole, blinds fit well in a contemporary setting, yet – made from heavy linen, damask or a pretty floral – they can be equally appropriate in a traditional room. Be imaginative with trims, too. Look for unusual pulls, from leather thongs to ceramic pebbles, and consider contrasting borders.

However modern the mood elsewhere at home, many people still prefer the softer look and enveloping feel of curtains in a living room. To look modern these days, curtains must fall in strong, sculptural folds and hang from simple poles, never fussy pelmets. When planning window treatments, remember the cost of fabric can really mount up. Plan for that. Interior designers always recommend using a cheaper fabric and getting drapes well made, rather than vice versa. Think about lining options. Interlining gives a particularly good drape and is a sensible choice if you live in chilly climes. If you like the unlined look but need privacy, then teaming unlined curtains with roller blinds is the ideal compromise.

Above If you like to watch the world go by, keep window treatments minimal: wooden shutters are very discreet.
Below left Investigate unusual curtain hangings, from stringing and eyelets to threading on suspension wires.
Below centre Plain contemporary curtains can be given a decorative twist with an inset panel, pin-tucked detail or a contrast leading edge.
Below right and opposite If privacy isn't an issue, use unlined sheers in plains or patterns to diffuse sunlight.

- **consider contrast linings**, from plain colours to a tiny floral print. This adds a decorative fillip to plain drapes, as well as looking pretty from the outside

- **curtains needn't be permanent**. Use a plain pole fitted with curtain clips for an ever-changing display, from bright sari lengths to an antique linen tablecloth

- **don't overlook ready-made high-street options**. The price differential between these and custom-made curtains or blinds can be substantial

- **dress curtains with plain roller blinds** will save on the amount of fabric required

storage & display

However busy it becomes in reality, the living room should have the potential to look tranquil and tidy. That's why great storage is crucial. Before deciding on storage styles, think long and hard about what really needs to be stored in the living room. Depending on the size of your home, it may be possible to relocate certain items – old photos or out-of-favour CDs – to the attic or basement. If space is tight, have regular clearouts. Things you keep in the living room should be items for enjoyment – music and books, treasures and mementoes.

Opposite and left For a truly tranquil space, devote one wall to custom-made storage, then conceal everything, from the TV to photo albums, with floor-to-ceiling doors.
Above left Even the smallest storage accessory can make a design statement. Look out for attractive magazine racks, storage boxes and CD racks.
Above right Plan living-room storage as an integral part of the room's design and the possibilities become more imaginative. This high-level bookcase includes dramatic lighting.

Above and below Rather than cram your shelves with possessions, think of their arrangement as an artform. **Above right** It pays to think about the sizes of your books before choosing shelves. In custom-made units, allow for low-level deep ones to hold coffee-table volumes, with lighter paperbacks higher up.

Built-in storage has the advantage of being tailor-made to suit your possessions, from book heights to TV size, and can match your chosen decorative style. Try to think beyond the conventional option of a bookshelf and cupboard in each fireplace alcove, which makes a room look smaller. Shelves can be fitted around a door, just below the ceiling, or spanning a bare wall. Closed storage options include a whole wall of panelling with individual doors that open to reveal cupboards; small alcoves inset into the wall, which hold everything from the TV to a vase; or shallow cupboards, wall-mounted or built into an alcove, with frosted glass, MDF or Perspex doors.

The advantage of freestanding storage is that it comes with you when you move. Don't just think of bookshelves; other options include mix-and-match units offering shelves and cupboards, traditional commodes or storage ottomans, sideboards or even plan chests. Inside each piece of furniture,

provide easy access to items like CDs and videos by placing them in cheap plastic racks, and keep bulky things such as photo albums low down so they are easy to lift out.

Plan where to house the technology at the outset, and the room will look slick. It's not an issue whether or not the TV is on show, but do try to conceal trailing wires. The video player doesn't have to sit directly below the TV and is more practically stored in a cupboard next to the stereo, near the videos and CDs. If you must have a computer in the living room, screen it carefully from the main sitting area.

Opinions differ as to whether books should, or shouldn't, be included in a living room. In a very elegant room, many

Above In a partitioned living area, add a 'window' with a shelf top to create an unexpected display area.
Left Long, shallow wall shelves provide the perfect opportunity for grouping family photos or artworks.
Below The sideboard has become a living-room essential, doubling up as a great storage option, with display space on top.

Right Particularly in tiny living rooms, it's essential that storage is decorative and multifunctional. This cabinet keeps CDs and videos in order, while providing the base for an unusual daybed.

Below left If you're lacking shelves, don't forget that pictures may be casually propped at floor level.

Below right You can't beat attractive storage boxes for keeping clutter at bay. But remember to keep the most frequently used items on the top of the pile.

Opposite Convert an unusual wall alcove – a redundant fireplace, for example – into dramatic storage.

colourful spines may spoil a rigid decorative scheme. In general, however, books add a lived-in, comfortable air. Spend time arranging shelves neatly – otherwise books quickly look messy.

The best living rooms bear the personality of their owner, so collect your favourite things here, be they serious artworks or stones gathered on the beach. Less is more in terms of display. A mantelpiece may need only a cluster of ceramic vases to look good. Pay attention to picture display, too. Instead of dotting paintings around the room, hang a cluster on a single wall – infinitely more arresting.

- which items really need to be stored in this room? Begin by **rationalizing your requirements**

- **think laterally about shelving** – it can be positioned in alcoves, across a wall, around a door or just below the ceiling

- however you store your TV or stereo, make sure any **trailing wires are concealed**

- **arrange shelves neatly**, mixing storage with display. Several broad-fronted shelves look fabulous propped with framed family portraits

- **less is more** – stamp your personality on the room with displayed items, but avoid clutter

putting it

together

Left While the contemporary look relies on boxy silhouettes and sharp corners, don't forget that a relaxing living room needs touches of softness too. A trendy fluffy rug or deep, welcoming upholstery does much to offset uncompromising modern lines.

Above Much new furniture is designed with a quirky twist, so look out for smaller items – from coffee tables to stools – with a sense of humour.

Opposite It's crucial to keep very modern rooms simple, but have fun repeating a chosen motif – a square, circle, triangle – in different ways. In this room, the square coffee tables and abstract canvases reinforce the cubic theme.

contemporary

The contemporary look is spawned by the uncompromising interiors of late '90s minimalism. Yet, if you prefer a more comfortable take on the modern look, there are plenty of style elements you can adopt. And who knows – the mantra of functionalism and order might just rub off a little.

Surfaces are vital to the contemporary look. Get these right and the other details will fall into place. The key is that they look expensive, even if they aren't. Of course, you can spend a small fortune on solid wood floors and polished plaster walls. But you don't have to. There are plenty of good-looking equivalents, like concrete or wood veneers laid over MDF, which cost half the price. And while you may need to invest in some new pieces of furniture, the sleek look, taken literally, needs only a few key pieces.

The ideal colour scheme is a variation on monochrome: white-on-white with natural tones or silvery metallics; or grey-on-grey, from graphite and gunmetal to pale blue-greys and off-whites. Soften these tones with accent colours, from lilac and scarlet, through to burnt orange, aubergine or citrus yellow, either in a piece of contemporary furniture, on walls or in cushions.

Above While hard surfaces are key to the contemporary look, save the concrete and marble for the kitchen. In the living room, add interest and colour with light-diffusing sandblasted glass, wood floors or glossy spray-painted units.

Right Though it looks cool and elegant, an all-white room runs the risk of seeming clinical. Adding one piece of furniture in a rich tone, such as a dark hardwood like Macassar ebony or wenge, warms it up considerably.

A rigorously designed modern interior requires careful choice of furniture. The high street is full of good copies of designer pieces in the essential boxy and slim silhouettes. Armchairs are square-shaped, while a sofa may be long and low to the ground or L-shaped. Team with these pieces glass- or stone-topped coffee tables and other furnishings in dark wood, brilliant gloss paint, lacquer or glass, all with stainless-steel detailing.

Fabrics need to be matt and slick, such as wools or leather, appropriate for the tight, figure-hugging silhouettes of sofas and chairs. Plains are most effective, but the odd graphic, geometric print can look good.

Above left Loft apartments are ideal backgrounds for the contemporary look, but their vast rooms and high ceilings need a practised eye to furnish. Soften long lean outlines with smooth curves and squashy beanbags to balance the space.

Above and left Display is vital to a strongly contemporary look, but keep it pared down. Use stark white walls for a gallery-like arrangement, and show off vases and accessories on shelves with with an almost sculptural minimalism.

smooth, sleek surfaces ...

capture the textures of gleaming glass, smooth stone and the confident gloss of lacquer

select **moody tones**, from graphite to gunmetal, biscuit to beige

cutting-edge rooms demand **streamlined surfaces and boxy furniture**

for modern elegance

sleek needn't mean uncomfortable: choose **luxurious upholstery**, such as wools, from flannel to bouclé, and alcantara, leathers and vinyls

store cherished accessories in built-in cupboards and choose one or two large-scale pieces for a **pared-down display**

Chaotic and noisy it may be, but family living is also sociable and fun. For parents and kids alike, there's incalculable merit to a living room where everyone can gather *en famille* or invite friends over for a get-together.

Great seating is crucial. Children love fun, versatile seating, particularly low-level options that can be drawn up to a coffee table for afternoon tea or for television-watching. Consider beanbags or seating cubes, which can look very sophisticated in leather or felt. Whatever the furniture, think robust rather than precious. You can help kids keep things tidy by filling your storage cupboards with smaller labelled boxes for toys. And keep plenty of space free on lower shelves for their books.

family-friendly

Opposite Kids love sprawling on the floor, so an unused fireplace is ideal for siting the TV at a low level. Have fun with living-room furnishings, using splashes of bright colour, either as rugs, cushions or upholstery.
Left Big sofas are great for sprawling on with friends, so pick a design that's long enough for gangly teenagers and upholstered in a cheerful, fuss-free fabric like cotton or denim that's easily cleaned.
Above and below When a living room doubles as a play space, there must be plenty of storage for quick tidy-ups. Here sturdy baskets, a retro sideboard and 1970s stacking compartments can all be stuffed with toys when playtime is over.

bisect the space in L-shaped or long narrow rooms to create a main social area and a quiet zone

children naturally gravitate downwards; **carpets or rugs** are soft on little knees (100 per cent wool cleans easily)

room to play & relax ...

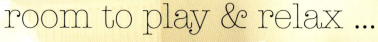

for all the family

conceal sticky fingerprints: painted walls can be touched up, while patterned or textured finishes hide marks

kids love **low-level seating** and the novelty of quirky furniture

ask your children what precious things they would like to include in the decor

country

The country look has cleaned up of late. Gone are the frills, the shiny chintz and the china ornaments. In their places have arrived rustic textiles, hard-working surfaces, and a faded colour palette, making the perfect backdrop for pretty antique pieces, from furniture to textiles. No matter if they are distressed or worn; what counts is that they are unique, decorative and functional.

Left and far left For a traditional country feel, pick baggy loose covers rather than tight upholstery, and play with mismatched stripes and checks – a perennial country classic.

Above and top Combine contemporary furniture with natural materials, from stone and wood to homespun upholstery, for a modern take on rustic style.

As a decorative style, the country look is low-maintenance and family-friendly. And, because it relies on a mixture of furniture styles, this is the ideal way to deal with hand-me-down furniture, junk-shop buys and possessions collected over the years. You won't need to buy new furniture; just sort through what you already have. And rigorous sorting is crucial – for country style, don't read jumble or clutter.

When choosing your decor, from wall surfaces to furniture, remember that they must look slightly battered or distressed; there's no place for spanking-new upholstery or garish gilding. So conserve rather than restore. There's a definite charm to a nineteenth-century sofa with its stuffing peeking out or to mirrors whose glass is gently foxed. And if you don't have the real thing, you can always fake it. Many a new pine table or door can be given the country look with watered-down vinyl matt paint, some wire wool and finishing wax.

Above For a modern take, pick wall panelling and wooden floors, but lighten them with white paint or pastel tones. Panelling styles can include tongue and groove or simple MDF squares.
Left If planning upholstery, replace fussy frilled detailing with more graphic scallops or box pleats, or a soft Greek-style buttoned mattress.

On walls, you can achieve the worn-out rustic look with dead-matt emulsion paint in faded shades, or for a truly earthy feel strip off all the wallpaper and leave the pretty patterns of the plaster underneath. Consider, too, the appeal of painted or unpainted brickwork. Wallpaper certainly fits in with the country look, but go for faded shades and avoid small or overly fussy patterns.

In terms of colour, it's not so much the exact shade you pick that matters, but the tone. Fresh pastels or any colours with too much white should be avoided in favour of washed-out or muddy tones. Instead of fresh white paintwork, choose one of the 'old' whites available from specialist paint ranges. Alternatively, experiment with woodwork in the same tone as the wall colour – always in eggshell, never gloss.

A tantalizing mix of textiles is a crucial part of country style. At the really traditional end, there are overblown faded chintzes, needlepoints, tapestries, patchworks and paisleys in classic patterns and textures. For a simpler look, choose ginghams, madras cottons and stripes, from ticking to deckchair canvas. Think about contrasting different textures, such as deep-pile velvet with tight-woven cottons. And mix your patterns with plenty of plain fabrics, which is the key to keeping the country look simple.

This page The focus of a country living room should be a welcoming sofa or daybed, piled high with cushions. The look is about mix and match, so contrast cushion sizes and shapes as well as patterns. Patchwork, the quintessential rustic textile, is becoming very trendy, with many attractive versions available on the high street.

relaxed in spirit, naturally tactile ...

nothing should appear new: your rooms should look naturally evolved

country style is inexpensive, and its **classic looks endure**

a **mix of textiles** is a key part of the rustic look – team faded chintz with ticking

country homes combine
**warmth, comfort and a
relaxed mood**

**fresh flowers, books and
candles** add to the ambience

if you're stuck for inspiration,
nature's tones provide the
perfect earthy palette

cosy & informal

Top Low-slung and slim, retro furniture is perfect for a trendy, chilled-out living room. For a more up-to-date sophisticated feel, stick to neutral upholstery.

Above It's fun (and still relatively cheap) to amass a collection of retro ceramics or lighting. Put it on display and let everyone enjoy it.

Right and far right So much of today's furniture has a retro feel that it's relatively easy to combine the two. Spice up plains with some abstract textiles or cushions. Or, for maximum impact, place a design classic chair centre stage and enjoy its fluid outline.

retro

It seems we can't get enough of the retro look. From '50s spiky-legged furniture to '70s floral fabrics, it looks good with today's modern shapes and spans an enticing colour spectrum, from hot brights to kooky pastels.

To steer your way through the retro maze, it's crucial to combine pieces with a sense of fun. And use them sparingly: a single kitsch '50s lamp is attention-grabbing, but choose too many battered pieces and the room will look like a twentieth-century museum. It is possible to buy new copies of classic designs, or you can search out stores which specialize in retro furniture. However, much more fun – and inexpensive – is to hunt down finds from junk shops.

raid **car-boot sales and junk shops,** even your parents' home – odds are that the coffee table you remember from childhood is a design classic now

the retro look isn't about period authenticity – have fun and enjoy the witty spirit in which many of them were designed

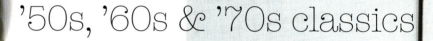

'50s, '60s & '70s classics

less is more: one retro chair and lamp can be all you need to give a funky new twist to a living room

use '50s and '60s fabrics as one-off cushions or stretched across a canvas for retro wall art

mix with sleek modern lines

Below If mixing across historical styles feels confusing, then stick to simple, symmetrical arrangements as a useful starting point.

Right Experiment with a mix of contemporary textiles and traditional furniture shapes. If you don't want to go the whole way and cover a Chesterfield in a Pucci print, then arrange cushions in modern abstract patterns against a plainly upholstered period sofa. Alternatively, cover a trendy new chair in a classic chintz.

Opposite There's a pleasing surprise factor in placing period furniture within a modern interior. Here, the contrast of leather and floral sofas in a whitewashed loft space creates a fresh and modern twist.

old & new

The freedom to mix across historical periods and decorative categories is guaranteed to provoke exciting and highly personal looks.

This style is all about contrast – a giant beanbag against Georgian wood panelling, a modern lounge-lizard sofa set beside vintage chintz curtains, or junk-shop finds displayed in a minimal gallery-like space. Whatever your style, aim for a fun, experimental mood, but to avoid the Miss Havisham cliché keep a tight rein on clutter. Mixing old and new is all about constant change, so when you bring the next great discovery home, put something else away.

always be on the lookout for new finds – the old & new style is **constantly evolving**

highlight the clash of antique and modern with quirky decorative touches

throw your possessions into sharp relief against a simple, gallery-like interior

a quirky & personal mix ...

can't be bought off the peg

'old' doesn't have to mean antique – instead, it may be **junk or second-hand**

'new' needn't be expensive designer acquisitions, it can be a **high-street bargain**

suppliers

Babylon
301 Fulham Rd
London SW10 9QH
020 7376 7255
www.babylonlondon.com
Danish mid-century pieces,
and own range

The Chair Company
60 Eden St
Kingston upon Thames
Surrey KT11 1EE
020 8547 2211
www.thechair.co.uk
Chair specialists

Coexistence
288 Upper St
London N1 2TZ
020 7354 8817
www.coexistence.co.uk
Re-editions and contemporary
furniture and lighting

The Conran Shop
81 Fulham Rd
London SW3 6RD
020 7589 7401
www.conran.com
Furniture, lighting
and accessories

Designers Guild
267–271 & 275–277 King's Rd
London SW3 5EN
020 7351 5775
www.designersguild.com
Exotic selection of
homewares, from hand-
thrown ceramics to fabrics
and contemporary furniture

Geoffrey Drayton Interiors
85 Hampstead Rd
London NW1 2PL
020 7387 5840
www.geoffrey-drayton.co.uk
Modern furniture

Nicole Farhi Home
17 Clifford St
London W1S 3RQ
020 494 9051
Exquisite accessories

Graham & Green
4 Elgin Crescent
London W11 2HX
020 7727 4594
www.grahamandgreen.co.uk
Furniture and accessories;
online shopping available

Habitat
0645 334433 for branches
www.habitat.net
Modern furniture, lighting and
home accessories

Heal's
196 Tottenham Court Rd
London W1P 9LD
020 7636 1666
Storage, furniture, lighting
and accessories

The Holding Company
241–245 King's Rd
London SW3 5EL
020 7352 1600
020 8445 2888 for mail order
Innovative storage solutions

Ikea
020 8208 5600 for branches
www.ikea.co.uk
Great value for Scandinavian-
designed furnishings

Inhouse
28 Howe St
Edinburgh EH3 6TG
0131 225 2888
Wide selection of modern design

Ligne Roset
0845 602 0267 for stockists
www.ligneroset.co.uk
Contemporary furniture
including modular sofas

Marks & Spencer
020 7268 1234 for branches
www.marksandspencer.com
Good value modern classics
from sofas to sideboards.
Online shopping available

McCord
0870 907 0870 for mail order
www.emccord.com
Furniture and accessories,
by mail order and online

Monsoon
020 7313 3000 for stockists
020 7313 4018 for mail order
www.monsoon.co.uk
Textiles and soft furnishings
with global influences

Muji
020 7323 2208 for stockists
Simple furniture, storage and
household accessories

Next
0116 286 6411 for stockists
and mail order
www.next.co.uk
Furniture and accessories

Ocean
0870 848 4840 for mail order
www.oceancatalogue.com
Furniture and accessories

Ochre
22 Howie St
London SW11 4AS
020 7223 8888
www.ochre.net
Furniture and lighting

The Pier
01235 821088 for branches
www.pier.co.uk
Inexpensive furniture
and accessories

Purves & Purves
220–224 Tottenham Court Rd
London W1T 7QE
020 7580 8223
www.purves.co.uk
Modern furniture, lighting
and accessories

Selfridges
Oxford St
London W1A 1AB
020 7629 1234
The Trafford Centre
Manchester M17 8DA
0161 629 1234
www.selfridges.com
Contemporary accessories
and furniture

Shaker
72–73 Marylebone High St
London W1U 5JW
020 7935 9461
Shaker-style accessories and
furniture, traditionally made;
mail order available

George Sherlock
588 King's Rd
London SW6 2DX
020 7736 3955
Traditional coil-sprung
upholstered sofas and chairs

Skandium
72 Wigmore St
London W1H 9DL
020 7935 2077
www.skandium.com
Modern Scandinavian design

Sofa Workshop
01798 343400 for branches
www.sofaworkshop.com
Classic and modern sofas

Viaduct
1–10 Summers St
London EC1R 5BD
020 7278 8456
www.viaduct.co.uk
Contemporary European
furniture and lighting

Vitra Ltd
30 Clerkenwell Rd
London EC1M 5PG
020 7608 6200
www.vitra.com
Furniture in classic
modern designs

credits

Key: ph= photographer, a=above, b=below, r=right, l=left, c=centre.

Endpapers ph Chris Everard/an apartment in Milan designed by Tito Canella of Canella & Achilli Architects; Page **1** ph Chris Everard/Ben Atfield's house in London; **2** ph Chris Tubbs; **3** ph Jan Baldwin/Interior Designer Didier Gomez's apartment in Paris; **4l** ph Chris Everard/a house in London designed by Helen Ellery of The Plot London; **4c** ph Jan Baldwin; **4r** Jan Baldwin/Jan Hashey and Yasuo Minagawa; **5** ph Andrew Wood/Mikko Puotila's apartment in Espoo, Finland, interior design by Ulla Koskinen; **6–7** ph Andrew Wood/David Jermyn's house in London, designed by Woolf Architects (020 7428 9500); **8** ph Chris Everard/Mark Weinstein's apartment in New York designed by Lloyd Schwan; **8–9** ph Chris Everard/an apartment in Milan designed by Tito Canella of Canella & Achilli Architects; **9** ph Andrew Wood/Alastair Hendy & John Clinch's apartment in London designed by Alastair Hendy; **9** illustration by Russell Bell; **10–11 & 11al** ph Andrew Wood/Rosa Dean & Ed Baden-Powell's apartment in London, designed by Urban Salon (020 7357 8800); **11ar** ph Chris Everard/an apartment in Milan designed by Tito Canella of Canella & Achilli Architects; **11br** ph Chris Everard/Adèle Lakhdari's home in Milan; **12** ph Jan Baldwin/Olivia Douglas & David DiDomenico's apartment in New York designed by CR Studio Architects, PC; **12–13** ph Chris Everard/an apartment in Paris designed by architects Guillaume Terver and Fabienne Couvert of cxt sarl d'architecture; **13a** ph Chris Everard/Mark Weinstein's apartment in New York designed by Lloyd Schwan; **13b** ph Chris Everard/Yuen-Wei Chew's apartment in London designed by Paul Daly Design Studio Ltd; **14al** ph Tom Leighton/interior designer Philip Hooper's own house in East Sussex; **14cl** ph Alan Williams/the Arbuthnott family's house near Cirencester designed by Nicholas Arbuthnott, fabrics designed by Vanessa Arbuthnott; **14bc** ph Chris Everard/Hudson Street Loft designed by Moneo Brock Studio; **14br** ph Alan Williams/Lindsay Taylor's apartment in Glasgow; **15al** ph Chris Everard/Pemper and Rabiner home in New York designed by David Khouri of Comma; **15ar** ph Alan Williams/Selworthy apartment in London designed by Gordana Mandic & Peter Tyler at Buildburo (www.buildburo.co.uk); **15bl** ph Alan Williams/New York apartment designed by Bruce Bierman; **15br** ph Catherine Gratwicke/Jonathan Adler & Simon Doonan's apartment in New York; **16** ph Catherine Gratwicke/Martin Barrell & Amanda Sellers' flat, owners of Maisonette, London; **16–17** ph Alan Williams/director of design consultants Graven Images, Janice Kirkpatrick's apartment in Glasgow; **17** ph Chris Everard/apartment in Antwerp designed by Claire Bataille & Paul ibens; **18l** ph Andrew Wood/the Kjaerholms' family home in Rungsted, Denmark; **18r** ph Jan Baldwin/Emma Wilson's house in London; **19** ph Andrew Wood/Michael Asplund's apartment in Stockholm, Sweden; **20a** ph Polly Wreford/an apartment in New York designed by Belmont Freeman Architects; **20b** ph Chris Everard/interior designer Ann Boyd's own apartment in London; **21al** ph Jan Baldwin/Jan Hashey and Yasuo Minagawa; **21ac** ph Andrew Wood/Roger & Fay Oates' house in Ledbury; **21ar** ph Chris Everard/Eric De Queker's apartment in Antwerp; **21b** ph Andrew Wood/a house in Stockholm, Sweden; **22l** ph Catherine Gratwicke/Francesca Mills' house in London, cushions from After Noah; **22ar** ph Polly Wreford/Louise Jackson's house in London; **22br** ph Polly Wreford/Clare Nash's house in London; **23l** ph Jan Baldwin/Clare Mosley's house in London; **23r** ph Catherine Gratwicke/Lulu Guinness's home in London; **24–25** ph Andrew Wood/Chelsea loft apartment in New York designed by The Moderns; **25l** ph Caroline Arber/Rosanna Dickinson's home in London; **25r** ph James Merrell; **26a** ph Catherine Gratwicke/Sasha Gibb, colourist, interior consultant and designer; **26bl** ph James Merrell; **26bc** ph Polly Eltes/a house in London designed by Charlotte Crosland Interiors; **26br** ph Henry Bourne; **27** ph James Merrell/an apartment in New York designed by James Biber of Pentagram with curtain design by Mary Bright; **28 & 29b** ph Andrew Wood/architecture and furniture by Spencer Fung Architects (020 8960 9883); **29al** ph Polly Wreford; **29ar** ph Andrew Wood; **30al** ph Catherine Gratwicke; **30ar** ph Chris Everard/David Mullman's apartment in New York designed by Mullman Seidman Architects; **30b** ph Jan Baldwin/Mona Nerenberg and Lisa Bynon's house in Sag Harbor; **31a** ph Jan Baldwin/interior architect Joseph Dirand's apartment in Paris; **31bl** ph Chris Everard/architect Jonathan Clark's home in London; **31r** ph Polly Wreford/Robert Merrett and Luis Peral's apartment in London; **32a** ph Chris Tubbs/Daniel Jasiak's home near Biarritz; **32bl** ph Henry Bourne; **32br** ph Andrew Wood; **33** ph Catherine Gratwicke; **34–35** ph Andrew Wood/Mikko Puotila's apartment in Espoo, Finland, interior design by Ulla Koskinen; **36** ph Chris Everard/Jo Warman – Interior Concepts; **37** ph Chris Everard/apartment in Antwerp designed by Claire Bataille & Paul ibens; **38l** ph Chris Everard/architect Jonathan Clark's home in London; **38r** ph Andrew Wood/Mikko Puotila's apartment in Espoo, Finland, interior design by Ulla Koskinen; **39al** ph Alan Williams/the architect Voon Wong's own apartment in London; **39ar** ph Chris Everard/an apartment in New York designed by Gabellini Associates; **39b** ph Chris Everard/an apartment in Milan designed by Tito Canella of Canella & Achilli Architects; **40a** ph Alan Williams/Alannah Weston's house in London designed by Stickland Coombe Architecture; **40b** ph Chris Everard/Ian Chee of VX design & architecture; **40–41a** ph Andrew Wood/a house in Stockholm, Sweden; **40–41b** ph Alan Williams/Stanley & Nancy Grossman's apartment in New York designed by Jennifer Post Design; **41ar** ph Andrew Wood/Christer Wallensteen's apartment in Stockholm, Sweden, lighting by Konkret Architects/Gerhard Rehm; **41b** ph Andrew Wood/Mikko Puotila's apartment in Espoo, Finland, interior design by Ulla Koskinen; **42l** ph Debi Treloar/architect Simon Colebrook's home in London; **42–43** ph Debi Treloar/Imogen Chappel's home in Suffolk; **43a** ph Debi Treloar; **43b** ph Debi Treloar/Eben & Nica Cooper's bedroom, the Cooper family playroom; **44l** ph

Debi Treloar; **44br** ph Debi Treloar /designed by Ash Sakula Architects; **44–45a** ph Debi Treloar/Catherine Chermayeff & Jonathan David's family home in New York designed by Asfour Guzy Architects; **45l** ph Debi Treloar/a family home in London, portraits by artist Julian Opie, Lisson Gallery; **45ar** ph Debi Treloar/Elizabeth Alford and Michael Young's loft in New York; **45br** ph Debi Treloar/The Zwirners' loft in New York; **46** ph Christopher Drake/designer Barbara Davis' own house in upstate New York; **46–47** ph James Merrell; **47a&b** ph Chris Tubbs/Nickerson-Wakefield House in upstate New York/anderson architects; **48l** ph Christopher Drake/Nelly Guyot's house in Ramatuelle, France, styled by Nelly Guyot; **48a&br** ph Chris Tubbs/Jonathan Adler and Simon Doonan's house on Shelter Island near New York designed by Schefer Design; **49l** ph Chrstopher Drake/Ali Sharland's house in Gloucestershire; **49a&br** ph Catherine Gratwicke/designer Caroline Zoob's home in East Sussex, selection of cushions made from antique fabrics by Caroline Zoob; **50** ph Simon Upton; **51al** ph Henry Bourne; **51bl&r** ph James Merrell; **51ar** ph Chris Tubbs/Clara Baillie's house on the Isle of Wight; **52al** ph Andrew Wood/Neil Bingham's house in Blackheath, London, chair courtesy of Designers Guild; **52bl** ph Tom Leighton; **52–53** ph Andrew Wood/Century (020 7487 5100); **53** ph Andrew Wood/Ian Chee of VX design & architecture, chair courtesy of Vitra; **54l** ph Andrew Wood; **54c** ph Chris Everard; **54–55** ph Polly Wreford/an apartment in New York designed by Belmont Freeman Architects; **55bl** ph Andrew Wood/Phillip Low, New York; **55 main** ph Polly Wreford/home of 27.12 Design Ltd., Chelsea, NYC; **55r** ph Polly Wreford; **56l** ph Chris Everard/Adèle Lakhdari's home in Milan; **56–57** ph Catherine Gratwicke/Laura Stoddart's apartment in London; **57** ph Polly Wreford; **58al** ph Tom Leighton; **58bl** ph Chris Everard/François Muracciole's apartment in Paris; **58–59** ph Polly Wreford/Ros Fairman's house in London; **59a** ph Andrew Wood/a house in London designed by Guy Stansfeld (020 7727 0133); **59bl** ph Catherine Gratwicke **59br** ph Catherine Gratwicke/Martin Barrell and Amanda Sellers' flat, owners of Maisonette, London.

Architects and designers whose work is featured in this book

27.12 Design Ltd.
+1 212 727 8169
www.2712design.com
Page 55 main

Jonathan Adler
+1 212 941 8950
Pages 15br, 48a&br

Elizabeth Alford Design
+1 212 385 2185
esa799@banet.net
Page 45ar

anderson architects
+1 212 620 0996
info@andersonarch.com
www.andersonarch.com
Page 47a&b

Arbuthnott
Nicholas Arbuthnott
Arbuthnott Ladenbury Architects
Architects & Urban Designers
15 Gosditch St
Cirencester GL7 2AG
and Vanessa Arbuthnott Fabrics
www.vanessaarbuthnott.co.uk
and Country House Walks Ltd
www.thetallet.co.uk
Page 14cl

Ash Sakula Architects
020 7837 9735
www.ashsak.com
Page 44br

Asfour Guzy Architects
+1 212 334 9350
easfour@asfourguzy.com
Pages 44–45a

Asplund (showroom and shop)
+46 8 662 52 84
Page 19

Claire Bataille & Paul ibens
+32 3 231 3593
bataille.ibens@planetinternet.be
Pages 17, 37

Belmont Freeman Architects
+1 212 382 3311
Pages 20a, 54–55

James Biber, AIA
Pentagram Architecture
204 Fifth Ave
New York, New York 10010
Page 27

Bruce Bierman Design, Inc.
+1 212 243 1935
www.Biermandesign.com
Page 15bl

Ann Boyd Design Ltd.
33 Elystan Place
London SW3 3NT
Page 20b

buildburo ltd
020 7352 1092
www.buildburo.co.uk
Page 15ar

Tito Canella
(Canella & Achilli Architects) Milan
+39 0 24 69 52 22
www.canella-achilli.com
Endpapers, pages 8–9, 11ar, 11br, 39b, 56l

Imogen Chappel
07803 156081
Pages 42–43

Jonathan Clark Architects
020 7286 5676
jonathan@jonathanclark
   architects.co.uk
Pages 31bl, 38l

Simon Colebrook
(Douglas Stephen Partnership)
020 7336 7884
www.dspl.co.uk
Page 42l

Comma
(David Khouri)
+1 212 420 7866
www.comma-nyc.com
Page 15al

Charlotte Crosland Interiors
020 8960 9442
www.charlottecrosland.com
Page 26bc

CR Studio Architects, PC
+1 212 989 8187
www.crstudio.com
Page 12

Fabienne Couvert & Guillaume Terver
cxt sarl d'architecture
+ 33 1 55 34 9850
www.couverterver-architectes.com
Pages 12–13

Eric De Queker
DQ – Design In Motion
Koninklijkelaan 44
2600 Bercham, Belgium
Page 21ar

Paul Daly Design Studio Ltd
0207 613 4855
www.pauldaly.com
Page 13b

Barbara Davis
+1 607 264 3673
Page 46

Dirand Joseph Architecture
+33 01 47 97 78 57
joseph.dirand@wanadoo.fr
Page 31a

Helen Ellery
The Plot London
020 7251 8116
www.theplotlondon.com
Page 4l

Gabellini Associates
+1 212 388 1700
Page 39ar

Sasha Gibb
01534 863211
home@sashagibb.co.uk
Page 26a

Ory Gomez
Didier Gomez
Interior Designer
15 rue Henri Heine
75016 Paris
+33 01 44 30 8823
fax. +33 01 45 25 1816
orygomez@free.fr
Page 3

Lulu Guinness
020 7823 4828
www.luluguinness.com
Page 23r

Nelly Guyot
Interior Designer &
Photographic Stylist
12, rue Marthe Edouard
92190 Meudon, France
Page 48l

Wendy Harrop
Interior Designer
11 Rectory Rd
London SW13 0DU
Page 50al

Alastair Hendy
Fax 020 7739 6040
Page 9

Philip Hooper
020 7978 6662
Page 14al

Interior Concepts
020 8508 9952
www.jointeriorconcepts.co.uk
Page 36

Jackson's
020 7792 8336
Page 22ar

Kjaerholm's
+45 45 76 56 56
www.kjaerholms.dk
Page 18l

Maisonette
020 8964 8444
maisonetteUK@aol.com
Pages 16, 59br

Francesca Mills
020 7733 9193
Page 22l

The Moderns
+1 212 387 8852
moderns@aol.com
Pages 24–25

Moneo Brock Studio
+34 661 340 280
www.moneobrock.com
Page 14bc

Clare Mosley
020 7708 3123
Page 23l

Mullman Seidman Architects
+1 212 431 0770
www.mullmanseidman.com
Page 30ar

François Muracciole
+33 1 43 71 33 03
francois.muracciole@libertysurf.fr
Page 58bl

Clare Nash
020 8742 9991
Pages 2, 22br

Mona Nerenberg (Bloom)
+1 631 725 4680
Page 30b

Roger Oates Design
01531 631611
Page 21ac

Jennifer Post Design
+1 212 734 7994
jpostdesign@aol.com
Pages 40–41b

Nico Rensch
www.architeam.co.uk
Page 45l

Lloyd Schwan/Design
+1 212 375 0858
lloydschwan@earthlink.net
Pages 8, 13a

Schefer Design
+1 212 691 9097
www.scheferdesign.com
Page 48a&br

Sharland & Lewis
01666 500354
www.sharland&lewis.com
Page 49l

Stickland Coombe Architecture
020 7924 1699
nick@scadesign.freeserve.co.uk
Page 40a

Urban Salon
020 7357 8800
Pages 10–11, 11al

VX design & architecture
020 7370 5496
www.vxdesign.com
Pages 40b, 53

Wallensteen & Co ab
+46 8 210151
wallensteen@chello.se
Page 41ar

Emma Wilson
www.45crossleyst.com
Page 18r

Voon Wong Architects
020 7587 0116
voon@dircon.co.uk
Page 39al

Woodnotes OY
+358 9694 2200
www.woodnotes.fi
Pages 5, 34–35, 38r, 41b

Woolf Architects
020 7428 9500
Pages 6–7

Caroline Zoob
Commissions 01273 479274
Caroline Zoob's work is also
available at:
Housepoints
020 7978 6445
Pages 49a&br

index